IMAGES
of America

CARBONDALE

Catholic Youth Center, Carbondale, Pa.   C-10

St. Rose/Sacred Heart High School. This 1950 postcard shows the newly constructed Catholic Youth Center/St. Rose High School, located on the corner of South Church Street and Seventh Avenue. This modern facility featured a swimming pool, bowling alleys, and a large gymnasium with seating for over 1,500 spectators. The building was the newest home for a school that began as St. Rose Academy in 1876 on Salem Avenue. In 1977, the name was changed to Sacred Heart High School, and it remained in operation until 2005, when despite a valiant campaign by students, parents, and alumni, it was closed by the bishop of Scranton. (Courtesy of the Carbondale Historical Society and Museum.)

On the Cover: The Light Yard crew of the Delaware and Hudson Railroad are assembled for this 1912 photograph. The Light Yard was where the empty freight cars and coaches were kept and maintained. These workers were responsible for coupling and uncoupling the cars, and they also performed basic repairs and maintenance. The pins that many of them are wearing on their caps or lapels are safety awards issued by the railroad. (Courtesy of the Carbondale Historical Society and Museum.)

IMAGES
of America

CARBONDALE

James J. Racht

ARCADIA
PUBLISHING

Published by Arcadia Publishing
Charleston, South Carolina

Library of Congress Control Number: 2010921763

For all general information, please contact Arcadia Publishing:
Telephone 843-853-2070
Fax 843-853-0044
E-mail sales@arcadiapublishing.com
For customer service and orders:
Toll-Free 1-888-313-2665

Visit us on the Internet at www.arcadiapublishing.com

To Marie, Zachary, and Juliette

CONTENTS

ACKNOWLEDGMENTS

The Carbondale Historical Society and Museum was established in 1975 and has worked tirelessly to preserve the rich history of the Carbondale area on a shoestring budget. This mission is carried out with some help from the City of Carbondale and through the herculean efforts of numerous volunteers as well as those of its executive director, Dr. S. Robert Powell. Dr. Powell's encyclopedic knowledge of local history was as important to the completion of this book as the photographs themselves, and I want to thank him for his invaluable assistance on this project.

In addition to the historical society's collection, other images were provided by the Lackawanna Historical Society, the Carbondale First United Methodist Church, Robert Vandenberg, Robert McDonnell of McDonnell's Restaurant, Chief Tom Brennan of the Carbondale Fire Department, Jim Muir of Mitchell Hose Company, Francis Sarnoski, John Uram, the Carbondale Public Library, Diane Kurlansky, and Ellen O'Malley Knavey, and I want to extend my heartfelt thanks to all of them for their assistance. Also, I want to thank my parents, Jule and Robert, and my brother, Nick, for instilling in me a love of history from a very early age. Thanks as well to my friends and business partners, Alex Kelly and Steve Rusin, whose patience and understanding were crucial to the completion of this project. Special thanks to my niece, Lydia Karnick, who enthusiastically promoted this book. I also wish to thank my editor at Arcadia Publishing, Erin Vosgien, for her guidance, patience, and support. And last, but certainly not least, I want to thank my wonderful wife, Marie, and our children, Zachary and Juliette, for their love and support.

Unless otherwise noted, all images are from the collection of the Carbondale Historical Society and Museum.

INTRODUCTION

In 1802, the area now known as Carbondale was called Ragged Island, and it was nothing more than a spot of unsettled wilderness along the Lackawannock Creek, which is how the Lackawanna River was then known. In this same year, a Rhode Island farmer named David Ailsworth was persuaded by his friend Capt. George Rix to settle in this remote part of northeastern Pennsylvania. In the spring of 1802, Ailsworth built a small log cabin and planted a single crop of corn. In the fall of that year, he moved his family down from Rhode Island, and the Ailsworths became the first permanent settlers in what is now known as the city of Carbondale.

In 1814, the Wurts brothers, William and Maurice, acquired some 70,000 acres of land in the region, which included most of the land on which Carbondale now sits. The Wurts brothers discovered that the area was rich in anthracite coal. They very rapidly established a mine and ultimately a railroad to transport the coal to New York City. A log house was constructed in 1822, which served as office, storehouse, bunk room, and tavern, and it was the first home of the Delaware and Hudson Canal Company. This company became a pioneering force in two major industries that would fuel the growth of 19th- and 20th-century America: anthracite coal mining and the railroads.

The growing industries needed workers, and European immigrants hungry for better lives flooded into the region and brought their diverse skills and cultures with them. Other industries sprang up to support the mines and railroads and to serve the rapidly growing population. Factories, foundries, textile mills, lumberyards, farms, shops, hotels, restaurants, and home builders all flourished during these years. Churches of many different denominations were founded and built. To serve the public, towns and cities were established, as well as civic organizations, schools, service and benevolent organizations, and labor unions. Opportunities for recreation grew with the establishment of parks, picnic grounds, camps, theaters, bands, sports teams, and clubs. Carbondale displayed its prosperity through the beautiful architecture found in its churches, commercial buildings, and Victorian homes, many of which still stand today.

Carbondale has been the birthplace and home of thousands of hardworking people who have served their community in both peace and war. Citizens have given their lives to defend the United States in every conflict since the Civil War. They have sacrificed at home as well, in the mines and breakers, on the railroads and in the factories, and protecting the homeland as police officers, firefighters, and members of the national guard. Among Carbondale's sons and daughters are those who went on to make a larger impact in the world and achieved notoriety beyond their hometown. Throughout this journey there have been many memorable events and interesting stories that have all contributed to the character of this city. And all of these things together—the industries, the people, the places, and the events—are what built this place and wrote this story, and they will continue to write new chapters as time marches on.

One

PIONEER CITY

From humble beginnings arose a thriving and bustling community whose fortunes rose and fell along with those of the nation that it helped to build. Carbondale grew quickly from these early beginnings and claimed the title of "Pioneer City" by being home to some significant firsts. Carbondale had the first deep underground shaft anthracite coal mine in the western hemisphere, and the first million-dollar corporation in the United States was the Delaware and Hudson Canal Company. The first steam locomotive to turn a wheel in the western hemisphere traveled on the Delaware and Hudson tracks between Honesdale and Carbondale. The first incorporated city in northeastern Pennsylvania, Carbondale has not only been home to industry but also to schools, churches, libraries, theaters, sports teams, performing arts, and civic organizations. All of these organizations and the people who built them come together to tell the story of this historic Pioneer City.

WILLIAM WURTS. By all accounts, William performed most of the Wurts brothers' preliminary explorations in the northeastern Pennsylvania wilderness during 1814–1815. According to a 19th-century history of the Lackawanna Valley, for two years the brothers "penetrated and bivouacked along the western range of the Moosic Mountains exploring every gorge and opening favoring the exit of coal . . . digging among rock and rattlesnake."

MAURICE WURTS. During one of his expeditions in the wilderness, Maurice came upon David Nobles, who was hiding in the woods to escape debtor's prison because he owed $15 to a creditor and was unable to pay. Maurice asked him if he knew of any coal in the area, and Nobles replied that he owned some land nearby where there were "curious black stones." He told Maurice that he would sell him the land if Wurts satisfied his $15 debt. Wurts wasted no time in satisfying Nobles's debt and purchasing his land, on which the Wurts brothers would ultimately establish their first coal mine.

THE OLD LOG TAVERN. This structure was built by the Wurts brothers in 1822. It served as an office, storehouse, bunkhouse, and tavern, and it is recognized as the first home of the Delaware and Hudson Canal Company. The building was located near where the Wurts brothers dug their first mine in the area, just west of the Seventh Avenue crossing of the former Delaware and Hudson tracks in Carbondale. This building was used by the company until it was torn down sometime around 1858.

BENJAMIN WRIGHT. The Wurts brothers' difficulty in transporting their first load of anthracite to market in Philadelphia during the winter of 1822–1823 (coupled with new coal interests being opened up in the Lehigh and Schuylkill areas) pushed the enterprising young company in a new direction. Benjamin Wright was the principal engineer building the Erie Canal, and the Wurts brothers enlisted his service to devise a plan to transport their coal from the mines in Carbondale to New York City. Wright served as the first chief engineer of the Delaware and Hudson from 1825 to 1827.

11

JOHN B. JERVIS. On March 14, 1827, the resignation of chief engineer Benjamin Wright was accepted, and his assistant engineer, John B. Jervis, was appointed to succeed him at an annual salary of $4,000. It was at this critical point that the decision was made to transport the coal from Carbondale to the canal at Honesdale via rail, and it was Jervis who was to make that vision a reality.

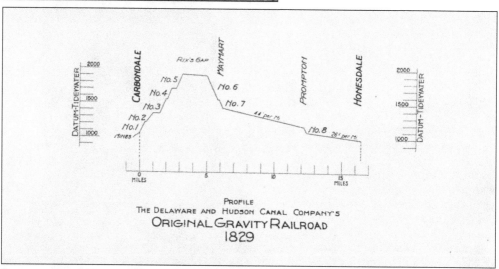

PROFILE OF THE GRAVITY RAILROAD IN 1829. This diagram shows the elevation of the original gravity railroad as it existed in 1829. The coal would be hauled up more than 900 feet of elevation in a distance of just over 3 miles. The cars would then coast in a controlled descent, powered only by gravity for the remaining 12 miles to the canal at Honesdale where the coal would be loaded on boats for the rest of its journey to New York City.

BANKNOTES OF THE DELAWARE AND HUDSON. On November 19, 1824, the New York State Legislature passed an act that granted the Delaware and Hudson Canal Company the right to exercise banking privileges. The company's bank opened for business at 13 Wall Street in New York City on June 27, 1825. Shown here are banknotes issued by the Delaware and Hudson Canal Company during the first half of the 19th century.

THE HONORABLE JAMES ARCHBALD. Born in 1793 in Ayrshire, Scotland, Archbald immigrated to the United States at the age of 12 and gained his first work experience on the Erie Canal. He was named the first superintendent of the gravity railroad in 1829. On March 15, 1851, the City of Carbondale was chartered by an act of the Pennsylvania Assembly. James Archbald was the first mayor of Carbondale, serving from 1851 to 1855. The borough of Archbald, which lies a few miles southwest of Carbondale along the gravity railroad line, is named in his honor.

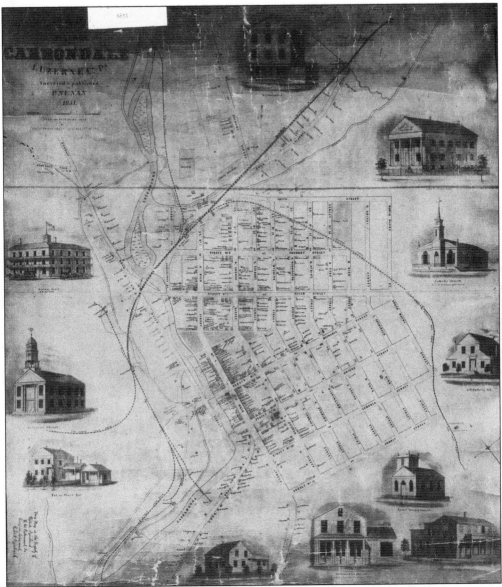

AN 1851 MAP OF CARBONDALE. P. Nunan was the surveyor and publisher of this map of the village of Carbondale, Luzerne County, in 1851. Since the map describes Carbondale as a village, apparently the map was finalized prior to March 15 of that year, which is when Carbondale was chartered as a city by the Pennsylvania State Assembly. This is the oldest known map of the city in existence, and like many maps of this era, it features illustrations of landmark buildings and the homes of prominent citizens. (Courtesy of the Lackawanna Historical Society.)

CARBONDALE IN THE 1860s. This image of the Pioneer City was taken looking east from a hill on the west side of the Lackawanna River in the 1860s. Some of the landmark buildings visible are the newly constructed city hall (left foreground), St. Rose of Lima Church (upper left), and

Trinity Episcopal Church (right foreground). The generous lots on which many of the houses stand are in sharp contrast to the tightly packed homes and businesses that still occupy the area to this day.

THE METHODIST EPISCOPAL CHURCH. Immediately after its chartering as a city in March 1851, Carbondale established a mayor's court, initially housed at the Methodist church on North Church Street near Salem Avenue. According to J. R. Durfee's 1875 book, *Reminiscences of Carbondale, Dundaff, and Providence*, the first trial held by the court was "a criminal case, a cross suit between the commonwealth and two Americans, two Irishmen, and two Negroes for an assault and battery." (Courtesy of the Carbondale First United Methodist Church and Robert Vandenberg.)

THE RAILWAY HOTEL. This detail from the 1851 map of Carbondale shows the Railway Hotel, which was run by a Mr. Porter. Of the four hotels in the city in the 1840s and 1850s, two were described in Durfee's book as "very respectable"—the Railway Hotel and the Mansion House, which was kept by David Blanchard. (Courtesy of the Lackawanna Historical Society.)

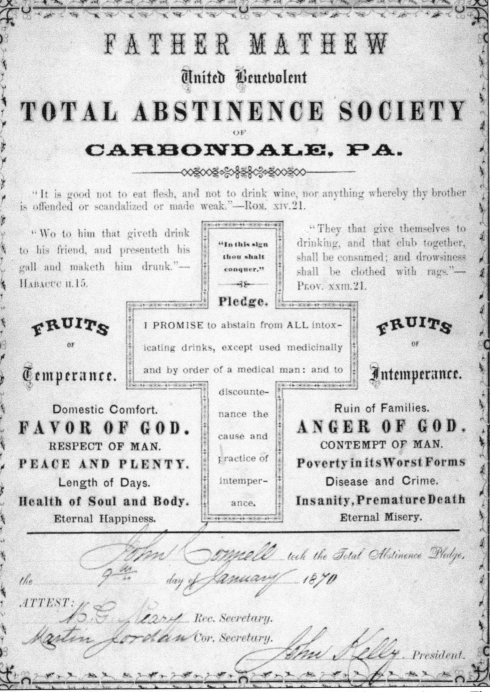

FATHER MATHEW

United Benevolent

TOTAL ABSTINENCE SOCIETY

OF

CARBONDALE, PA.

"It is good not to eat flesh, and not to drink wine, nor anything whereby thy brother is offended or scandalized or made weak."—ROM. XIV.21.

"Wo to him that giveth drink to his friend, and presenteth his gall and maketh him drunk."— HABACUC II.15.

"In this sign thou shalt conquer."

"They that give themselves to drinking, and that club together, shall be consumed; and drowsiness shall be clothed with rags."— PROV. XXIII.21.

Pledge.

I PROMISE to abstain from ALL intoxicating drinks, except used medicinally and by order of a medical man: and to discountenance the cause and practice of intemperance.

FRUITS OF **Temperance.**

Domestic Comfort.
FAVOR OF GOD.
RESPECT OF MAN.
PEACE AND PLENTY.
Length of Days.
Health of Soul and Body.
Eternal Happiness.

FRUITS OF **Intemperance.**

Ruin of Families.
ANGER OF GOD.
CONTEMPT OF MAN.
Poverty in its Worst Forms
Disease and Crime.
Insanity, Premature Death
Eternal Misery.

John Connell took the Total Abstinence Pledge,

the _____ 9th _____ day of *January* 1870

ATTEST: *H. G. Leary* Rec. Secretary.
Martin Jordan Cor. Secretary.
John Kelly, President.

ABSTINENCE PLEDGE. Temperance societies were very popular in 19th-century America. The Father Mathew Total Abstinence Society was founded by a Catholic priest in Ireland in the early 1800s. The large influx of Irish immigrants to the city resulted in the Carbondale chapter of the society being founded on September 11, 1868. As of 1874, the organization had 307 members.

COLUMBIA HOSE COMPANY No. 5. Although it bears the number five, Columbia Hose Company is the oldest fire company operating in Carbondale. Founded in 1856, the company operated out of this two-story brick structure located beside city hall until the late 1970s. In this 1965 photograph, Jack Loftus (left), Joe Dougher (center), and Joe Healy are seen outside the company quarters on a Sunday morning. (Courtesy of Tom Brennan.)

COTTAGE HOSE COMPANY No. 2. This volunteer fire company was organized in 1894 and bears the number two because it was the second company founded after the fire department's restructuring in the early 1890s. The company was reorganized in 1972 as Cottage Hose Ambulance and still provides fire and emergency medical services to the area today.

ANDREW MITCHELL HOSE COMPANY NO. 1. Founded in 1892 during a reorganization of all the city's fire companies, the Mitchell Hose Company took the name of a local businessman and community leader who was instrumental in the reorganization. In this 1964 photograph, the company's old horse-drawn fire truck appears in a parade, driven by Russ Cliff and Bill Burrell. Records show that the two original draft horses who served the company were named Dan and Diamond. (Courtesy of the Andrew Mitchell Hose Company and Jim Muir.)

KLOTS FIRE BRIGADE. In the 19th and early 20th centuries, it was very common for larger businesses to have their own fire departments. In the days before automatic sprinkler systems, this was viewed as a necessity by many business owners—fire was the single biggest threat to their operations. The Klots Throwing Company was a silk mill that moved to Carbondale from New York City in 1894 after a fire destroyed its operation there.

CARBONDALE HIGH SCHOOL CLASS OF 1901. This graduating class poses in front of the high school, which was built in 1847 and was the main high school in Carbondale until it was replaced by a much larger high school in 1916. The number of graduates was relatively small because most students left school to begin working to help support their families long before graduation.

ST. ROSE ACADEMY CLASS OF 1930. In September 1876, the Sisters of The Immaculate Heart of Mary established a convent and school on Salem Avenue in the city near the present-day Marian Community Hospital. The school was supported by St. Rose Parish, and it was given the name St. Rose Academy. Over the years, the school has had several different names and has been located in several different buildings.

STUDENTS OF PUBLIC SCHOOL No. 9. This elementary school was located on Park Street near Tenth Avenue in the city's southeast side. Letha Kunkle served as principal and is presumably one of the women looking out the window in this *c.* 1920 photograph.

EMERGENCY HOSPITAL NURSING SCHOOL GRADUATES. This is a group of graduating nurses in 1902; the nurse on the far right is Ora Loomis. For much of the city's history, Carbondale was home to two hospitals and nursing schools. The emergency hospital, which later became the general hospital and the city hospital, went on to become St. Joseph's Hospital. (Courtesy of Robert and Donald Powell.)

CARBONDALE HIGH SCHOOL FOOTBALL TEAM. To this day, Carbondale's high school has a football team. For many years, St. Rose Academy and High School also fielded a team. This photograph depicts the Carbondale High School team in 1911.

ST. ROSE BASKETBALL TEAM. In addition to football, basketball has also always been a popular high school sport in Carbondale. Here is the 1932 St. Rose squad. Standing fifth from the left in this picture is Frank Howard, who would go on to serve as mayor of Carbondale from 1960 to 1968. Notice how these basketball players are wearing more protective padding than their modern counterparts, while the football players in the above photograph are wearing noticeably less.

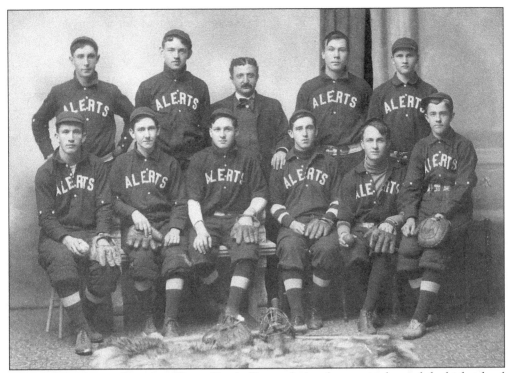

CARBONDALE ALERTS BASEBALL TEAM. Baseball's popularity always went beyond the high school and college fields in the late 19th and early 20th centuries. Large companies such as a railroad or manufacturer would frequently sponsor amateur baseball teams. Though not much is known about the Carbondale Alerts, the man standing in the center of this photograph has been identified as the Honorable Abraham Sohm, mayor of Carbondale from 1908 to 1912.

CARBONDALE PIONEERS BLUES. This semiprofessional minor league team was affiliated with the Philadelphia Phillies organization until the late 1940s. They played their home games at Russell Park and were league champions in 1947. After the team lost its minor league status, it still continued on as an amateur team for several years.

THE MOZART BAND. Marching bands were very popular during the late 19th and early 20th centuries. In addition to the bands organized by many organizations, such as the Boy Scouts, the Salvation Army, and various fire companies, there were also a number of independent community bands. The Mozart Band was one such group in Carbondale; they were founded around 1876 and continued on well into the 1930s.

OPERA HOUSE CAST. The cast of a production at the Grand Opera House on Main Street poses onstage for a photograph after a performance. The opera house was one of several theaters in town that not only staged local productions but also hosted touring companies as well. These performances covered a wide range of entertainment genres from opera to vaudeville.

PATRIOTIC PERFORMERS. These star-spangled dancers from a 1920 production of *Oh! Oh! Cindy* are posing for a photograph behind the United Methodist church. Given the location chosen for the photograph, one can assume that this was a church group production, a fairly common event during this time period.

CARBONDALE HIGH SCHOOL ORCHESTRA. In this 1929 photograph, one can further see the important role music and the performing arts played in the lives of Carbondale's people. For a small public high school, a 31-piece classical orchestra is an impressive accomplishment.

CIVIL WAR MONUMENT. When duty called, the citizens of Carbondale always responded. A large number of them served in the Civil War, many with the 143rd Pennsylvania Infantry. After the war, the parade ground located across from city hall was turned into a memorial park. This monument was the park's first, erected in 1885 and accompanied by a flagpole and a large fountain.

DELAWARE AND HUDSON WELCOME HOME ARCH. World War I was no different than previous wars for the people of Carbondale. Many first-generation Americans stepped forward to defend their nation in 1917. In the summer of 1919, the Delaware and Hudson Railroad erected this arch over North Main Street near the company's offices to welcome home all the troops, especially their employees who had left their jobs to serve.

DRAFTEES DEPARTING IN 1943. Duty called yet again in World War II, and once more Carbondale sent its youth to defend freedom. Carbondaleans would serve with honor and distinction on every front in the war from North Africa to Normandy and from the Pacific to Italy. This group of Carbondale draftees is preparing to depart from the Lackawanna Railroad Station in Scranton.

THE HOME FRONT. Those who stayed behind during the war did their part as well, including the two Civil War cannon that had been stationed in Memorial Park since the 1880s. These two artillery pieces were cut up and donated during one of the many wartime scrap metal drives that were run throughout the country. The two cannon would have the honor of serving the United States in two wars.

THE CARBONDALE CYCLE CLUB. There have been many different recreational groups in Carbondale throughout history, and here one of these groups poses proudly on Main Street with their state-of-the-art Harley Davidson motorcycles. This photograph is believed to be from around 1920, and one of the club members is known to be Clell Anderson.

SWIMMERS. Carbondale has been geographically blessed with close proximity to a lot of water. Streams, rivers, ponds, lakes, reservoirs, swimming holes, and waterfalls have always abounded in this region. Swimming has always been a very popular summertime activity, and here are four gents from the early 1900s sporting the latest swimming fashions of the day.

PIONEER BOY SCOUTS. The Boy Scouts of America was founded in 1910, and true to Carbondale's pioneer traditions, the city was quick to embrace the movement. Here is a large group of scouts, from what is likely Troop No. 2, posing in front of the new post office on Main Street in 1911.

YOUNG RUNNERS. Another activity that has been enjoyed by children for generations is running. Here is a group of youngsters at the start of a 1-mile race in June 1909. They are about to head out north on Main Street in front of city hall. The Anthracite Hotel is behind them—take note of the brick road surface and trolley tracks.

RIDING THE TROLLEY. One of Carbondale's earliest forms of public mass transportation was the trolley. Here is a crowded car on Main Street in front of city hall in the late 1880s. The side of the car reads, "Carbondale and Jermyn Street Railway, Carbondale, Glenwood, and Jermyn." This trolley service likely operated between Carbondale and the two communities located southwest of town: Glenwood (later known as Mayfield) and Jermyn. (Courtesy of the Lackawanna Historical Society.)

THE CARBONDALE KIWANIS CLUB. In this 1920s photograph, members of the Carbondale Kiwanis Club pose in front of the post office with a group of young scholarship winners. The Kiwanis Club is one of many community service organizations that have served the city and its residents for decades, and it still does so to this day.

Two

THE BIRTHPLACE
OF ANTHRACITE

Being in the manufacturing business in Philadelphia, William and Maurice Wurts were looking for a good source of anthracite, or stone coal as it was commonly called. The fledgling industries of the young United States were primarily dependent upon imported bituminous coal from England. However, during the War of 1812 the supply of this precious fuel was all but cut off. The enterprising brothers felt that anthracite presented a wonderful opportunity, not only for American fuel independence, but also for great personal wealth.

The brothers found substantial outcroppings of anthracite on land that they owned in what would later become Carbondale. These outcroppings were the exposed sections of huge veins of coal that led deep under the earth to what would later become known as the Northern Anthracite Coal Fields. They opened the first underground anthracite mine in the United States near what is now Seventh Avenue and Mill Street in June 1831. This would be the first of a multitude of mines that would produce millions of tons of coal over the next 130 years.

First Underground Mine Marker. The plaque on this monument reads in part, "The first underground anthracite mine opened here June 1831 by Archbald Law, first mining engineer of The Delaware and Hudson Canal Company, John Wurtz, Pres." The marker was erected in 1901 in honor of the city's 50th anniversary, and it still sits just west of the Seventh Avenue crossing.

COAL MINERS. Here a group of coal miners stands near a mine entrance, ready to begin the day's work, around 1890. Many of the men are wearing flowers pinned to their shirts or hats. The flowers may be to demonstrate support for unionization; this was a common, nonverbal way for the workers to express their solidarity in the early days of the organized labor movement.

INTERIOR OF A MINE. This photograph shows a somewhat idealized version of the interior of a coal mine—the well-cleared chamber, adequate lighting, and evenly spaced supports make the environment seem quite reasonable. This photograph and the next three are from an early 1900s booklet entitled *A Trip Through the Anthracite Mines.*

MINERS AT WORK. This somewhat more realistic depiction of work in an anthracite mine shows the miner boring a hole for the blasting charge while the laborer loads a car with chunks of coal that had been loosened by previous blasting and digging.

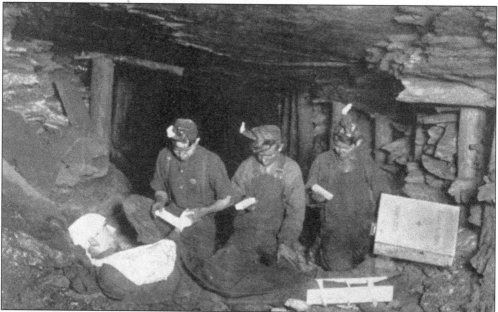

MINE FIRST AID. This photograph from the mine series depicts a group of miners administering first aid to an injured coworker. Revolutionary new first aid techniques were first developed in the Carbondale area by Dr. Matthew Shields of Jermyn in 1899. These practices would eventually be adopted by mines and many other industries throughout the world and were taught and promoted by the Red Cross.

THE MULE AND MOTOR CAR. These two images show the evolution of mine transportation. At the beginning of their work day, the miners would ride the empty cars into the mine and to the chambers where they would be working. These cars would then be used to haul the coal out during the course of their shift, and at the end of the day the last cargo the cars would carry would be the miners themselves. In the early days, the mine cars were pulled by mules, which were eventually replaced by electric motorcars as the technology became more sophisticated.

WORK AT THE BREAKER. Here one can see the process that the coal went through after it left the mine. It was hauled up to the top of the breaker and dumped in, after which it moved through several different processes. The coal would be broken down into smaller pieces of various sizes. All of the rock shale and debris would be picked out of the coal by the "breaker boys," as shown in the picture below. Then the coal would be washed and moved to final storage areas or coal pockets where it would be readied for shipment.

RACKET BROOK AND COAL BROOK. There were several prominent coal breakers or collieries in Carbondale during the height of the anthracite mine industry from the 1830s through the 1930s. These are photographs of the Racket Brook Breaker and Coal Brook Breaker, which were both owned by the Delaware and Hudson Company's mining operation, the Hudson Coal Company. The Coal Brook Breaker was the largest and most prominent facility because it was centrally located right next to the Delaware and Hudson Railroad yard.

THE ERIE AND POWDERLY. The coal breakers were the face of the coal mines not only due to their massive size but because they were the only part of the operation easily visible to the public. The lives of the miners and their families were centered around the breakers because that is where the men worked, where they received their pay, and where they gathered in times of tragedy and celebration. In the photograph below is a patriotic celebration and a Liberty Bond rally at the Powderly Breaker in 1918.

COAL COMPANY ADVERTISEMENT. Coal began to steadily lose its share of the home heating market in post–World War II America. Here is a promotional brochure for Delaware and Hudson anthracite from the early 1950s. This marketing campaign showed the latest in coal furnace and thermostat technology being used in new, modern homes. Despite their efforts, the coal industry would continue to steadily lose customers to oil, natural gas, and electric heat.

STRIP MINING. In later years, underground mining gave way to strip mining, where large machines known as drag lines would drag huge steel buckets across the ground and literally strip away the layers of earth covering the coal seams. This technique was embraced by the industry because it was cheaper, safer, and required far less labor. The downside was that the hillsides were left looking like a barren moonscape.

ABANDONED DEANGELIS BREAKER. As the coal industry declined, the carcasses of abandoned breakers became another common sight in coal country. These once-bustling centers of a mining community would be left behind to rot once a mine operation shut down. Areas that once had thriving coal mines were littered with abandoned breakers in the 1960s and 1970s. These hulking structures were dangerous playgrounds for bored youngsters and scavengers looking for scrap metal or machinery.

TWO KINDS OF FIRE. These photographs show two ways in which fire was a special hazard to the residents of a coal mining community. A breaker fire almost always resulted in the total destruction of the structure because they were primarily wood structures covered with coal dust and full of lubricants for the machinery. This was also the ultimate fate of virtually every abandoned coal breaker in the anthracite region. A mine fire was a particularly difficult problem for two reasons: it was underground and it had a huge supply of fuel. Mine fires would usually start when rubbish thrown into a pit being used as a makeshift landfill was ignited either intentionally or by accident. If this trash fire was close enough to an exposed coal seam, it would ignite the coal, and the fire would follow the seam down into the mine.

MINE SUBSIDENCE. Another unique problem facing the residents of a mining community was the mine subsidence or cave-in. In areas such as Carbondale, where underground mining had been going on for over 100 years, the earth was a spider web of underground tunnels. Many of these chambers had been long abandoned, and over time the timber supports would give way or flooding would wash away pillars, and huge holes would open up in the earth without warning. Some of these openings were large enough to cause entire houses to drop 20 feet down into old mines.

THE END OF AN ERA. This image of the lower part of St. Rose Cemetery with the Powderly Breaker and railroad cars in the background accurately foretells the fate that would soon befall these two industries that helped build Carbondale and the United States over the course of 150 years.

Three

THE RAILROADS

Necessity is the mother of invention; this is certainly true in the case of the birth of the Delaware and Hudson Railroad. The Wurts brothers found a huge source of anthracite coal, centrally located between the New York and Philadelphia markets. The problem was that nearly 100 miles of mountains and wilderness lay between their coal and these two port cities.

Their first plan was to ship the coal by boat to Philadelphia via the various natural waterways that existed between the two. After only one shipment, this was determined to be impractical due to the distance and the shallow waters that existed at various points along this route. Another obstacle to the Philadelphia market was the fact that new coalfields were being developed in the Lehigh Valley much closer to Philadelphia. This development led the fledgling young company to ship their coal via rail over the Moosic Mountains to Honesdale where it would be loaded onto boats and taken via canal to the Hudson River and ultimately New York City.

Once the rail line was completed to Honesdale, the company tested one of two steam locomotives that they had purchased from England for use on the line. This locomotive was known as the *Stourbridge Lion* and was placed on the rails in Honesdale on August 8, 1829, for a 6-mile, round-trip test run. This was the first locomotive to turn a wheel in the western hemisphere. After a second test run on September 9, it was determined that the locomotives were too heavy to be used safely or efficiently on the railroad at that time. The company engineers decided to instead use the challenges of this mountainous terrain to their advantage and design a gravity railroad system. Engine houses were built at several points on the route between Carbondale and Honesdale, and the cars would be towed up the incline by the use of heavy ropes or chains. They would then descend, propelled by gravity and their own weight, with the speed controlled by a brakeman. After unloading their cargo in Honesdale, they would make the return trip in the same manner. It is in this way that the Delaware and Hudson Canal Company's railroad was born. The railroad operated trains from Carbondale, transporting both freight and passengers for the next 140 years.

THE *STOURBRIDGE LION* AND HORATIO ALLEN. Above is the first steam locomotive to ever operate in the western hemisphere, and to the left is the man who was at the controls for this historic trip. After the *Lion*'s only rail trips in August and September 1829, it was removed from the rails and eventually wound up in the Delaware and Hudson shops in Carbondale, where its boiler was removed and put to use as a generator. The boiler eventually wound up at the Smithsonian Institution in Washington, D.C., and Allen continued to have a very successful engineering career until his death in 1889.

PLANE NO. 2 ENGINE HOUSE AND SHEPHERD'S CROOK. The boilers in the engine house provided all the power needed to haul the freight and passenger cars up the steep inclines of the Moosic Mountains. The power for the descending legs of the journey was all provided by Mother Nature. The passenger cars in the picture below are coasting around the bend that gave this section of the gravity road its nickname, Shepherd's Crook.

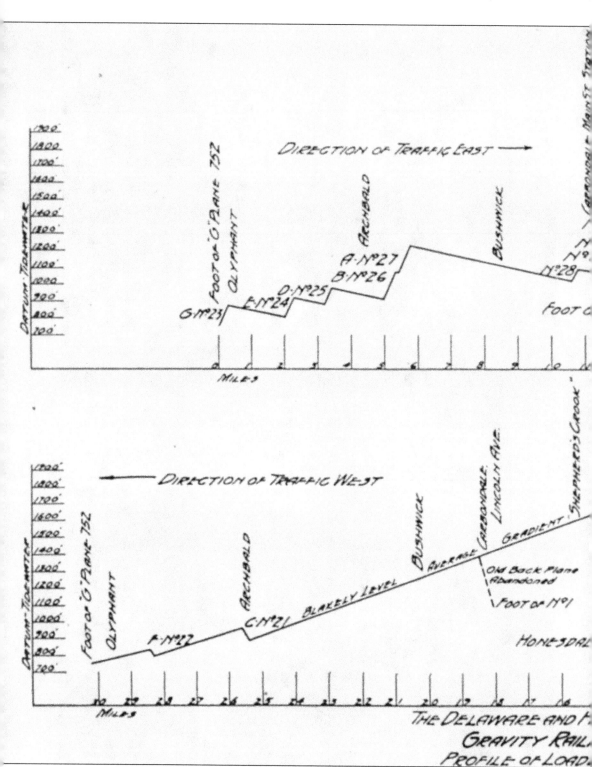

GRAVITY RAILROAD PROFILE. This profile illustrates the elevations of the gravity railroad's loaded and light tracks as they existed from 1866 until the railroad ceased being a primarily

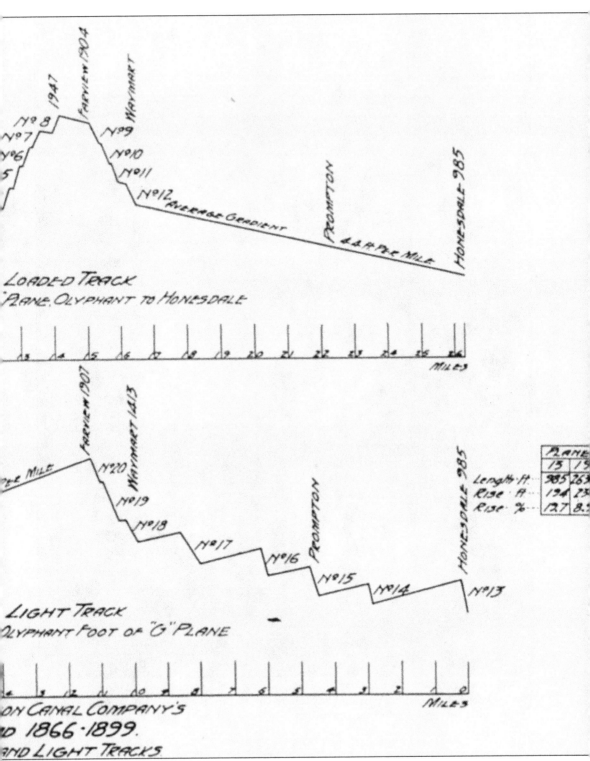

LOADED TRACK
"J"PLANE. OLYPHANT TO HONESDALE

LIGHT TRACK
OLYPHANT FOOT OF "G" PLANE

ON CANAL COMPANY'S
D 1866·1899.
AND LIGHT TRACKS

gravity-powered enterprise in 1899.

A Beehive of Activity. Here is a typical workday scene at the gravity railroad shops in the late 1800s. Dozens of workers are busy building and repairing cars, passengers can be seen boarding a train in the background, and the whole area is awash in car parts and tools.

PLANES NOS. 10 AND 20 ON THE GRAVITY ROAD. These two images show some of the intricate engineering details found on the railroad. In the photograph above, the contraption to the right is a counterbalance used to maintain tension on the tow lines used for ascent. In the image at right, the angled rails attached to the main rails are a derailer used to remove runaway cars from the tracks before they crash into cars further down the line.

Delaware and Hudson Pay Car Passaic. In this stereoscopic image from the 1880s, a company pay car is stopped along the line near Archbald, southwest of Carbondale. The men gathered are likely workers ready to collect their wages.

The Last Gravity Passenger Train. This is the last gravity passenger train to leave Carbondale bound for Honesdale. It was December 1899, and the train pulled out of Carbondale at 3:00 p.m. The conductor was Ed Hubbard. The following month, the company began to convert the gravity line over to an entirely locomotive-powered line.

DELAWARE AND HUDSON ENGINE NO. 2, C. P. WURTS. This type 4-4-0 engine was built to the gravity rail gauge of 4 feet, 3 inches in 1860. The engine was rebuilt in the Carbondale shops in November 1873 and sold to the Dickson Locomotive Works in Scranton in 1874.

DELAWARE AND HUDSON ROUNDHOUSE, 1870s. This was the first roundhouse built in the Carbondale yards. Constructed in 1871, it has been referred to as the "lower roundhouse" because it was located near the southern end of the yard.

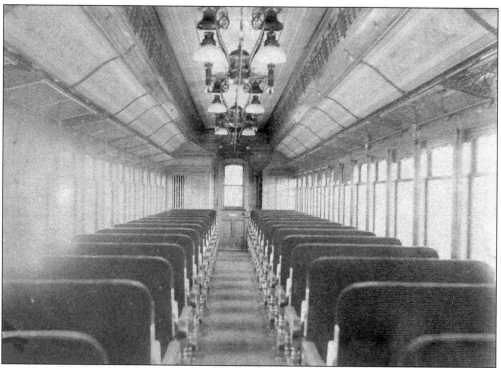

DELAWARE AND HUDSON PASSENGER CAR AND CAR SHOPS. Here is a photograph of the interior of a brand-new passenger car constructed in the Carbondale car shops in 1898. The image below shows the interior of the car shops with workers putting the finishing touches on another passenger car.

DELAWARE AND HUDSON CAR BUILDING CONTEST. The idea to use competitions to improve employee morale and productivity is not a new one. In the above photograph a team is working on a freight car outside the shop building. Notice the bleachers with spectators to the right. The photograph below shows the winning team from such a competition posing in front of their car with their trophy.

DELAWARE AND HUDSON YARD, 1932. This view of the Carbondale yard was taken in 1932. The photographer was standing on the Dundaff Street viaduct, and much of the yard can be seen

from this vantage point. A work gang is visible near the center of the photograph, and the Coal Brook Breaker can be seen in the distance to the left.

DELAWARE AND HUDSON PASSENGER STATION. Sometimes referred to as the Seventh Avenue Station and located near the intersection of Seventh Avenue and River Street, this building was constructed in 1896 and continued to serve passengers of the railroad until 1952. This beautiful building then sat abandoned until it was destroyed by fire in the 1970s.

DELAWARE AND HUDSON ROUNDHOUSE, 1920. This structure was built in 1884 to replace the 1871 roundhouse. This was the largest roundhouse constructed in the yard and had the capacity to house 57 locomotives. This was also the last roundhouse built in the yard, and it operated until the yard closed down in the 1950s. This massive structure slowly deteriorated over the next 40 years and was finally demolished in the 1990s.

INSTALLING THE NEW TURNTABLE. In 1926, the Delaware and Hudson needed to upgrade their roundhouse turntable to accommodate larger and heavier engines. Because of the critical importance of the turntable in the daily operation of the railroad, this massive undertaking had to be completed in one day.

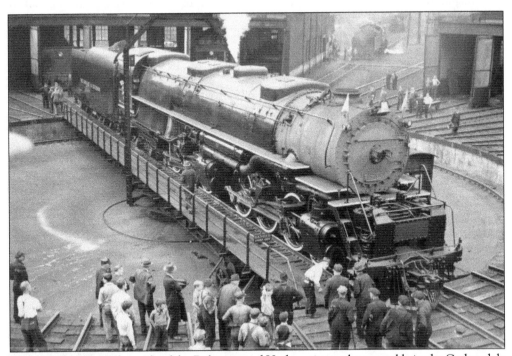

ENGINE No. 1502. The pride of the Delaware and Hudson sits on the turntable in the Carbondale roundhouse in July 1940. This engine was the largest locomotive in the company's fleet, and it barely fit on the turntable.

RAILWAY FREIGHT AND AGENTS. In the days before UPS and FedEx, the railroad was the main mode of land transportation for all the commercial freight in the world. The picture above shows a group of freight agents on an educational trip in 1926; these were the men responsible for moving this freight. In the picture below is one of the larger items of freight moved by the railroad—a World War I–era field artillery piece.

STEAM POWER AND TRAIN WRECKS. Delaware and Hudson engine No. 536 speeds along the rails pulling a load of freight cars in the above 1937 photograph. Accidents on the railroad were inevitable, and collisions between trains were particularly messy affairs. Pictured below is the wreckage left after the collision of two passenger trains in September 1912.

DUNDAFF STREET VIADUCT. Constructed in February 1922, the viaduct was built in order to elevate the roadway over the Delaware and Hudson tracks at the southern end of the Carbondale yard. The rapid increase of automobiles on the road led to this project, an attempt to allow vehicular traffic and the still-busy rail yard not to interfere with each other. The viaduct remained in use until it was finally removed in the 1980s.

NEW DELAWARE AND HUDSON OFFICE CONSTRUCTION. This 1927 photograph shows the construction of a new railroad office building on North Main Street in front of the original company shops. The railroad offices were housed in these buildings until the 1950s. One building was left vacant and was eventually demolished some years later; the newer building still stands today and is home to a popular local restaurant.

DELAWARE AND HUDSON PAINTING CREW. At its peak, the railroad was by far the biggest employer in the city, and its employees engaged in a broad range of trades. Here is a group of painters from the 1930s; these men were kept continually busy not only with painting the various rolling stock, but also with the upkeep of railroad buildings and signage as well.

MACHINISTS IN TRAINING. Also much in demand on the railroad were the machinists who repaired and maintained the locomotives, as well as all the other mechanical equipment used in the daily operation of the company. This photograph from around 1910 shows a group of apprentice machinists at the Delaware and Hudson shops.

MEMBERSHIP AWARD. This award was issued to master mechanic Thomas M. Murphy of Carbondale on the occasion of his 50th anniversary as a member of the Brotherhood of Locomotive Enginemen and Firemen. Murphy was the car and locomotive foreman in charge of the Pennsylvania division of the Delaware and Hudson.

GANDY DANCERS. The crews responsible for maintaining and repairing the railroad tracks were known as gandy dancers. When working locally, they would use a small electric car for transport, like the one shown above, but if they had to go on an extended trip they would often travel and live in a caboose for the duration of their trip.

DIESEL POWER. As the years went by and new technologies were developed, steam locomotives gave way to diesel engines. The diesels had no need for coal and water and were able to operate more efficiently over longer distances with smaller crews.

DELAWARE AND HUDSON CABOOSE. The locomotives were not the only things modernized by the railroads; the iconic red caboose also received an update as well. The modern caboose in the diesel era was outfitted with the latest in radio communications and electronic signaling equipment in order to improve railroad safety.

LAST TRAIN FROM SCRANTON. At 5:20 p.m. on January 4, 1952, the last Delaware and Hudson passenger train to Carbondale left Scranton. Driven by Lewis Davis, engine No. 500 arrived at 6:00 p.m., marking the end of more than 100 years of passenger train service in Carbondale.

DIESEL WRECKS. Even with new technology, many of the same old problems persisted. The improved efficiency of the diesel locomotives did nothing to help trains stay on the rails, as illustrated by the above photograph. The wreck shown in the photograph below is a perfect metaphor for the battle between the locomotive and the automobile: although the train looks as if it won this battle, the truck would ultimately win in the end.

MODERN DIESELS. Although passenger service had ended, freight trains were still a regular sight in the Carbondale area throughout the 1960s and 1970s. Here is an example of two types of diesel engines that pulled those freight trains. The above photograph shows a Delaware and Hudson engine of that time period with its trademark blue, gray, and gold colors. The photograph below is of the Delaware and Hudson engine 1776, the *Spirit of Freedom*, which was painted red, white, and blue in honor of the U.S. bicentennial in 1976.

HISTORY ERASED. After sitting vacant for many years, two icons of the railroading history of Carbondale and of the country were destroyed. The Delaware and Hudson Seventh Avenue passenger station was destroyed by fire in the 1970s, and the original gravity railroad shops were demolished to make room for a parking lot in the 1980s. Although the buildings have not survived, it is important to continue to work to preserve the memory of these places and their significance in the industrial history of this country.

Four

OTHER BUSINESSES
AND INDUSTRIES

As the home of two major industries—coal mining and the railroad—Carbondale naturally attracted other supporting industries such as lumber mills, foundries, and textile manufacturers. All of this industry had a tremendous thirst for labor, and thousands of people immigrated to the area and made it their home. This rapid population growth led to the rise of other businesses, such as butcher shops, groceries, dry goods, pharmacies, clothing stores, hardware stores, hotels, restaurants, and theaters, just to name a few.

This economic growth made Carbondale a commercial center in the region. In the early years, the railroad and mines paid their employees in cash. This also led to the founding of several local banks, which continued the commercial growth of the city. To this day, Carbondale is still home to a wide variety of business ventures, some of which are almost as old as the city itself.

HENDRICK MANUFACTURING COMPANY. Founded in 1876 by Eli E. Hendrick, the company was a pioneer in the perforated metal industry. Eli Hendrick had an industrial background, having been in both the mining and oil-refining businesses. The above picture shows the original Hendrick offices along Dundaff Street. The photograph below shows a horse-drawn delivery sleigh carrying one of the company's early products. The company is still engaged in the same line of business and is still located in Carbondale to this day.

HENDRICK WORKERS. This group photograph of the Hendrick employees was taken around 1890 outside of the company shops. The company was fortunate that their products had a wide variety of uses in many different industries, and it grew rapidly as the demand for their products was driven by industrial growth throughout the nation.

DEFENSE AWARD. In addition to the private sector, Hendrick also became a major government contractor. In 1943, they received a prestigious defense department award for excellence in manufacturing. Here the plant is seen decorated for the award ceremony, which was attended by high-ranking military and political officials.

AERIAL VIEW OF THE HENDRICK COMPLEX. From the 1940s through the 1960s, Hendrick was at its peak as far as size and production were concerned. This photograph shows the sprawling company complex as it occupied both sides of Dundaff Street. The Ontario and Western railroad

trestle cuts diagonally across the frame, and the Delaware and Hudson tracks are running along the bottom of the photograph. Many of these buildings are still in use today by other businesses. The Hendrick Company built a new plant and offices nearby and relocated there in the 1970s.

CENTRAL LABOR UNION. This organization represented a variety of tradesmen, such as painters or bartenders, who did not belong to one of the major mining or railroad unions of that time. The Central Labor Union was founded in 1900, and this photograph was taken in front of the post office in 1925 at their annual convention, where they celebrated the organization's 25th anniversary.

GENTEX EMPLOYEES. The Klots Throwing Company was a silk and textile mill originally founded in New York City. After a fire destroyed their building in New York, they relocated to Carbondale in 1894 primarily to be in close proximity to the booming railroad and mining industries. The company eventually changed its name to General Textiles and finally Gentex, as they became more involved in defense-related work during World War II. To this day, the company is still a major defense contractor and one of the larger employers in the Carbondale area.

J. B. VAN BERGEN AND COMPANY. Established in 1833 for the principal purpose of casting wheels for the Delaware and Hudson Railroad, Van Bergen and Company was originally known as the Reed and Gurney Foundry and was located on Foundry Street (now Lincoln Avenue) between Church and Main Streets. After changing ownership and names several times over the years, it eventually became known as J. B. Van Bergen and Company in 1873 and shortly thereafter relocated to Dundaff Street.

THE CARBONDALE MACHINE COMPANY. This company was founded in 1899 by several managers from Hendrick Manufacturing with financial backing from Eli Hendrick. Their main line of business was the design and manufacture of refrigeration and later air-conditioning equipment. The above picture shows a display of some of the company's equipment. The photograph below features a group of managers and company salesmen taken at their annual convention in 1922. The Carbondale Machine Company operated independently until 1934 when it was sold to the Worthington Pump Company. The company operated as a subsidiary of Worthington until 1949, at which time all local assets of the company were liquidated.

OUTDOOR WORKERS. Another major industry in the Carbondale area that was a major supplier to the mines and railroads was the lumber industry. Several lumber mills in the area kept very busy supplying mine support timbers, railroad ties, construction lumber, and telegraph/utility poles. Based on the tools of their trade, the young men in this photograph are either lumberjacks or utility pole workers.

THE JERMYN BLOCK. This stereoscopic image from the 1880s shows the area of Salem Avenue between Main Street and the Lackawanna River. The large Italianate structure in the middle was known as the Jermyn Block because it was built by prominent businessman John Jermyn as a home for the local Masonic Lodge, which rented out the ground floors as commercial space. The two structures on either side of the lodge are still home to various retail shops today.

MOSES AND ROEMMELMEYER. The above photograph, taken in 1878, shows Mr. Moses on the left and his new young partner, Mr. Roemmelmeyer, on the right. After the retirement of Moses, the store became known only as Roemmelmeyer's and continued in the same location on Main Street for the next 100 years. The photograph below shows what the storefront looked like in the early 1920s after being updated.

TIME MARCHES ON. The landmark clothing store underwent another face-lift in the late 1930s, giving it an art deco look more fitting for the time period. This is how the storefront looked for the remainder of its existence until it closed down for good toward the end of the 20th century.

VON BECK WINES AND LIQUORS. This establishment was located on Seventh Avenue in the area of Mill Street. It is believed that it was more a saloon than a wine store as they are known today. Owner John P. Von Beck stands in the doorway in this 1880s photograph; the two young boys are his sons George P. and John M., who were later the operators of Von Beck Brothers Hardware and Plumbing store in Carbondale. (Courtesy of Diane Kurlansky.)

MEAT AND PRODUCE. Like many small communities in America at the time, Carbondale had a very self-contained economy, and this is illustrated by these two photographs. Above is E. M. Casterline's butcher shop and grocery, and below is Reynold's store, displaying a large quantity of fresh produce. Most stores would specialize in one type of product, but invariably they all carried an array of other products as well. For example, the produce seller in the photograph below has a sign in the window advertising "24 kinds of ladies and gents underwear."

DRUGGIST AND DRY GOODS. This photograph shows J. S. Jadwin's store near the intersection of Main Street and Salem Avenue. Jadwin's was a drugstore and book shop, but as the signage suggests, his inventory was quite diverse. The image below shows a shopkeeper at the counter of his dry goods store.

BANKING. All of the industrial and commercial activity in Carbondale created a need for banking services; consequently, the city has had several banks operating simultaneously for most of its history. The First National Bank of Carbondale, pictured at left, was organized in November 1864 and is the oldest financial institution in town. The building in the picture was constructed in the 1920s at the corner of Main Street and Salem Avenue and still houses the bank today, although it has changed names and ownership a few times. The picture above shows the interior of the Liberty Savings Bank around 1920. This building was located at the corner of Church Street and Salem Avenue, and it also houses a bank to this day.

LODGING AND ENTERTAINMENT. Other businesses well represented in the city throughout its history have been hotels and theaters. The above photograph shows a guest room of the Anthracite Hotel, which was located at the corner of Main Street and Sixth Avenue across from city hall where the current Carbondale Fire Department headquarters is. The photograph below shows the Majestic Theatre on the corner of Main Street and Seventh Avenue in 1951. This building also had a large hall on the second floor that was frequently used for basketball games, boxing matches, and dances.

KRANTZ BREWERY. Peter Krantz poses here with the employees of his brewery around 1893. Krantz purchased the brewery from Loftus and Nealon in 1889. In 1897, the brewery became part of the Pennsylvania Central Brewery, which was a co-op of 13 breweries. The Krantz Brewery remained in operation until Prohibition. (Courtesy of Robert McDonnell.)

PHOTOGRAPHY. Several professional photography studios made their home in Carbondale over the years, and two of the most prolific were those of Cramer and Yarrington. Families would routinely sit for formal portraits in the photographer's studio to mark important events such as weddings and baptisms, but the photographers would also go to their clients as well. This image shows a young family posing on the front porch of their new home; a coal breaker can be seen in the background.

THE BUSINESS DISTRICT. These two postcard views show the variety of business concerns that crowded the downtown of Carbondale in the early 20th century. Virtually every enterprise is represented: hotels, restaurants, groceries, clothing stores, dry goods, theaters, drugstores, hardware stores, municipal government, and transportation. In the photograph below one can see the trolley tracks running through the snow. This was prototypical Main Street America, where residents could have all of their needs met just a few minutes' walk from their home and workplace.

EATING ESTABLISHMENTS. Servers stand at the ready behind the counter of this soda fountain in the 1930s. Every block in the business district seemed to have at least one restaurant, diner, luncheonette, or ice cream shop in residence during the first half of the 20th century.

AUTO SERVICE. As automobiles became more common on America's city streets, so too did service stations. This is Whitey's Service Station at the corner of Main Street and Lincoln Avenue in the 1940s. Part of the first floor also housed Cino's Photography Studio, and at one time the Kingdom Hall of Jehovah's Witnesses occupied the second floor.

Five

NOTABLE PEOPLE

Carbondale, like many communities in the United States, is a collection of immigrants of many different nationalities, religions, ethnic groups, social classes, and life experiences. This diverse mix of people has produced many citizens of distinction and accomplishment. The citizens of Carbondale have proudly spilled their blood, sweat, and tears not only to build, improve, and protect their city but also their country. Most of Carbondale's early settlers were not even born in the United States, but they made it their home and recognized the unique and precious opportunities that their new home afforded them. They worked hard to secure not only a better life for themselves but a better life for their children and grandchildren.

This book is not long enough to recognize everyone who made a contribution, and many of those names and deeds are lost to history. A few people have been selected from different backgrounds and vocations who achieved great things and made this community a better place. This is an attempt to represent the many who contributed much with a few.

Sgt. Patrick Delacey. While serving with the 143rd Pennsylvania Infantry during the Civil War, Delacey earned the Congressional Medal of Honor for his heroic actions during the Battle of the Wilderness in Virginia on May 6, 1864. However, he was not actually awarded the medal until September 1894. (Courtesy of the Carbondale Public Library.)

MSGR. THOMAS COFFEY. One of the most beloved pastors of St. Rose of Lima Parish, Monsignor Coffey would serve from 1887 until his death in 1925. He was the first pastor of the parish who was not born in Ireland, and under his guidance the church building was enlarged and renovated in 1900. He is presently interred just outside the main entrance to the church and is the only person buried on church grounds.

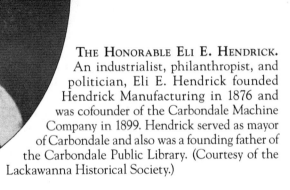

THE HONORABLE ELI E. HENDRICK. An industrialist, philanthropist, and politician, Eli E. Hendrick founded Hendrick Manufacturing in 1876 and was cofounder of the Carbondale Machine Company in 1899. Hendrick served as mayor of Carbondale and also was a founding father of the Carbondale Public Library. (Courtesy of the Lackawanna Historical Society.)

THE HONORABLE TERRANCE V. POWDERLY. Born in Carbondale to Irish Catholic immigrants in 1849, Powderly began as a switch tender with the Delaware and Hudson Railroad. He would later become a machinist and organized labor activist and go on to serve as mayor of Scranton, Pennsylvania, from 1878 to 1884. Powderly succeeded Uriah Stephens as the leader of the Knights of Labor from 1879 until 1893 and later served as U.S. commissioner general of immigration, appointed by Pres. William McKinley. (Courtesy of the Lackawanna Historical Society.)

SECOND LT. JOSEPH R. SARNOSKI. While serving with the 43rd Bomber Group in the Pacific in June 1943, Sarnoski volunteered to serve as bombardier on very dangerous reconnaissance mission. When his aircraft fell under attack by 20 enemy fighters, he manned the nose guns of the aircraft and ferociously defended the plane, allowing the pilot to complete the mission. Even after being severely wounded, he continued to fight off the attacking planes and shot down two of them before he succumbed to his wounds and collapsed on his guns. (Courtesy of Francis Sarnoski and the Carbondale Public Library.)

PATROLMAN WILLIAM F. MCANDREW. The only Carbondale police officer to be killed in the line of duty, officer McAndrew was shot while trying to stop an armed robbery in Dickson City in 1913. This memorial to him is located in front of city hall on Main Street, and the inscription includes the quote, "The Valiant never Taste of Death but Once."

WINIFRED MURRAY RAU. Known on stage as Wynn Murray, this Broadway actress and singer was born in Carbondale in 1920. She starred in such popular musicals as *Babes in Arms*, *The Boys From Syracuse*, and *Sons O' Fun Revue*. She also toured with the USO during World War II and was injured in New Guinea during a Japanese bombing raid. She died February 6, 1957, and is buried at Arlington National Cemetery.

Nicolai H. Hiller. Born in 1868 in Siberia to a Russian mother and an American father who worked in the shipping industry, Nicolai was raised in New York City and received a degree in engineering from the Stevens Institute. He came to Carbondale in 1889 to work for Hendrick Manufacturing and was one of the founders of the Carbondale Machine Company, serving as its president. He was an active civic leader and philanthropist, serving on the board of the Carbondale Public Library and the Pioneer Dime Bank and helping to charter the local Red Cross chapter and serving as its chairman. He was also very active in the Trinity Episcopal Church. In his later years, he became an avid painter and photographer of nature. He passed away while attending a Stevens alumni event in New York City at the age of 95. (Courtesy of the Carbondale Public Library.)

GEN. JEROME F. O'MALLEY. Born in Carbondale in 1932, Jerry O'Malley graduated from St. Rose High School in 1949 and the U.S. Military Academy at West Point in 1953, choosing a commission in the U.S. Air Force. As a pilot he flew 116 combat missions in Vietnam. He also flew the first operational mission of the legendary SR-71 "Blackbird" at speeds of over 2,000 miles per hour. He rose through the ranks, serving as vice chief of staff and commander in chief of Tactical Air Command. At the peak of his career, he and his wife were tragically killed in a plane crash at the Wilkes-Barre/Scranton International Airport on a trip back home to speak at a Boy Scouts anniversary dinner. To this day, the U.S. Air Force has two officer awards named in honor of the O'Malleys. (Both, courtesy of Ellen O'Malley Kanavy.)

Six

HISTORIC PLACES

A community is nothing more than the sum of its people and their deeds. The structures that they build and the places they preserve are monuments to their memory and reminders to those who follow to keep moving forward and reaching higher so that they too might leave this place better than they found it.

Although some of the places covered in this chapter no longer exist, fortunately, many of them do. People can still visit places that have witnessed virtually the entire life of this city and the lives of those who built it. All of these places have a story to tell, and that story continues to be written.

CARBONDALE CITY HALL AND COURTHOUSE. After the original wooden structure burned down in 1859, it was replaced the following year by a brick edifice. The 1860 building more than doubled in size after an extensive addition in the early 1890s. This three-story addition included the entire front half of the building, featuring its signature clock tower and archway entrance.

ST. ROSE OF LIMA. Home to a congregation established in 1832 by Irish-Catholic immigrants, the St. Rose of Lima Catholic Church seen here was the parish's third home in this same location. This particular building was constructed in 1872, and it was extensively enlarged and renovated in 1900.

OUR LADY OF MOUNT CARMEL. This church's congregation was formed by Italian immigrants in the early 1880s and held its services in a small wood-frame structure on the corner of Brown and Villa Streets. The building pictured here was erected in 1900; the first Mass was held on Christmas of that year and presided over by Fr. Anthony Cerrutti.

99

CARBONDALE FIRST UNITED METHODIST CHURCH. Founded in 1828, this is one of the oldest congregations in Carbondale. The present building was constructed in 1892 and completely gutted by fire less than 10 years later. The church was immediately rebuilt with construction being completed in 1903. This congregation was the mother church in the Wyoming Conference of Methodist churches.

FIRST PRESBYTERIAN CHURCH. Established in 1829 by the Hudson Presbytery, this congregation's original home was a small one-room building on the present site. In 1836, a larger, more formal structure was erected to replace the original building. This served as the congregation's home for the next 115 years. On June 3, 1951, the large stone Gothic structure pictured here was officially dedicated.

BEREAN BAPTIST CHURCH. Organized in 1848, this congregation originally met in a small building located between St. Rose's and the Methodist church. After some time, a new church building was constructed on the corner of Lincoln Avenue and Church Street. It was severely damaged by fire on August 21, 1968. The congregation decided to rebuild at the same location, and the newly restored church was dedicated on September 13, 1970.

TRINITY EPISCOPAL CHURCH. This congregation was formed in 1832, and they purchased a share in the newly built Methodist church, which they used on alternate Sundays. In 1839, they sold their share in the church and began plans to erect their own building. The original structure was completed in 1842 on River Street near Sixth Avenue. This served as their home until a new church was built on the same property in 1901. The current church features magnificent stained-glass windows made by Tiffany and Company in 1899.

CARBONDALE PUBLIC LIBRARY. The Young Men's Library Association was incorporated in January 1875 and was located in the Delaware and Hudson offices on North Main Street. In 1895, it was moved to city hall. The structure pictured here was built by Bell Telephone Company, which moved out in the early 1960s. At that time, several prominent citizens purchased the building to be used as the new home for the library. The library remained at this location on the corner of Church Street and Sixth Avenue until a new library was built next door to city hall in the late 1990s.

CARBONDALE HIGH SCHOOL. Constructed in 1847, this school building was destroyed by fire in 1916. At the time of its construction, it was the only high school in the city. By 1923, Carbondale had one public high school, one parochial high school, 10 public elementary schools, and one parochial elementary school. Today things have come full circle, and there is just one high school, one public elementary school, and one parochial elementary school.

BENJAMIN FRANKLIN HIGH SCHOOL. Constructed in 1916, Benjamin Franklin High School was just being completed when the old Carbondale High School it was replacing was destroyed by fire. Located on Lincoln Avenue between Terrace and Wyoming Streets, it remained in service until it was replaced by the present-day Carbondale Area Junior-Senior High School in 1976.

JOHN MARSHALL PUBLIC SCHOOL NO. 8. Located on Belmont Street near Maple Avenue, this school was built in 1900 and remained in use for nearly 75 years. For many of those years, its principal was legendary Carbondale educator Alice V. Rashleigh. (Courtesy of Robert McDonnell.)

ST. JOSEPH'S HOSPITAL. In 1926, the Sisters, Servants of the Immaculate Heart of Mary took over the operation of the Carbondale City Hospital located on Washington Street and moved the hospital to their convent and school facilities near the top of Salem Avenue. They also changed the institution's name to St. Joseph's Hospital. This 1950 postcard shows the hospital building that was completed in 1929 at a cost of $500,000. After several additions and renovations over the years, this hospital is still operating under the name Marian Community Hospital.

CARBONDALE EMERGENCY HOSPITAL AND NURSING SCHOOL. The Carbondale Hospital Association was chartered in 1889, and this hospital was constructed at a cost of $21,000. On May 1, 1893, the hospital opened its doors to the public, and it remained at this location on Hospital Street until 1931.

CARBONDALE GENERAL HOSPITAL. The Hudson Coal Company purchased the land on which the Carbondale Emergency Hospital sat in exchange for another, larger parcel of land a short distance away on Fallbrook Street. The Carbondale General Hospital was erected on this site and opened its doors in 1933. This facility remained in operation until 1992, when it merged with St. Joseph's Hospital and consolidated operations at the St. Joseph's site under the new name of Marian Community Hospital.

CARBONDALE YMCA. Built in 1914 on North Main Street across from the Delaware and Hudson offices, the YMCA has been providing area youth with recreational and educational opportunities ever since. The association is still operating at this facility, and it has just finished a huge $10 million expansion and renovation project.

THE IRVING THEATRE. Of the two movie theaters that shared Carbondale's Main Street for decades, the Irving was always known as the upscale theater. The photograph above shows the interior of this beautiful venue, which opened in 1923, featuring its own house orchestra and hosting vaudeville acts. A sound screen was installed in 1928, and the theater became primarily a movie house, showing popular first-run films of the day. The picture below depicts a huge crowd gathered outside waiting to be admitted in 1939 to see Don Ameche in *Alexander Graham Bell*. The theater remained in operation until the 1960s, and it was eventually torn down. (Both, courtesy of Robert McDonnell.)

THE GRAND OPERA HOUSE AND HOTEL AMERICAN. This early 1900s postcard shows the Grand, the American, and the Shannon Building lining the west side of Main Street between Salem and Lincoln Avenues. The hotel was built in 1893 and replaced the smaller American House Hotel that had stood in its place. An advertising slogan for the hotel declared it to be "Where the Poconos Meet the Catskills."

ANTHRACITE HOTEL. This massive brick Victorian structure was an iconic fixture in the center of Carbondale for almost a century. Being located across the street from city hall and close to the Delaware and Hudson Railroad Station, scores of travelers passed through the Anthracite regularly. The building was ultimately destroyed by fire in the early 1970s. (Courtesy of Robert McDonnell.)

ODD FELLOWS HALL. Built in 1846 and dedicated on July 4 of that year, this building is one of the oldest in Carbondale, standing at the corner of Church Street and Seventh Avenue. Founded in England in the late 18th century, the Independent Order of Odd Fellows was the first civic organization established in Carbondale. (Courtesy of the Lackawanna Historical Society.)

U.S. POST OFFICE. Constructed in 1911, the beautiful classical architecture of this structure and its central location on the corner of Main Street and Lincoln Avenue made this one of the most photographed buildings in the city. As is illustrated by several of the photographs in this book, the most popular place to have a group photograph taken was on front steps of the post office. The post office was located here until it was replaced by a new building in the 1980s.

ARCHITECTURAL DETAIL FROM THE
PIONEER DIME BANK. An example of some
of the beautiful and unique architecture
found in many of Carbondale's older
buildings can be seen here on either
side of the facade of the former Pioneer
Dime Bank. The intricate detail in the
stonework is further highlighted by
the oversized replica of an actual dime
embedded in the design, with each replica
displaying a different side of the coin. It
was said that the "coins" were actually
plated with silver or some other precious
metal. Today this building is home to
the Greater Carbondale Chamber of
Commerce; the "coins" were removed
some time ago by a previous owner.

GRAVITY PARK. Tucked away alongside Racket Brook behind a few residential buildings near the intersection of Terrace Street and Garfield Avenue is a little park that memorializes the beginning of a big era. The focal point of this park is a white obelisk that commemorates the Delaware and Hudson Gravity Railroad. There is a plaque on the monument that indicates it was erected in 1923 in celebration of the 100th anniversary of the Delaware and Hudson Company.

HENDRICK ESTATE. This 1870s engraving shows the E. E. Hendrick estate located along what is now Lincoln Avenue just below Laurel Street. The main house was originally built on this 10-acre park in 1852 as the home of Charles P. Wurts, president of the Delaware and Hudson Company. Hendrick purchased the property in the 1870s, and it remained in the family for the next 120 years. The property has been subdivided over time, but the main house remains a private residence.

MEMORIAL PARK. Originally known as the parade grounds, this empty land was used for decades by grazing animals or drilling militiamen. It was not until 1885 when the Grand Army of the Republic erected a memorial to casualties and veterans of the Civil War that it officially became Memorial Park. A large flagpole and ornate Victorian fountain were also installed. Today the fountain is gone, but other memorials have been added over the years, keeping with the park's tradition of remembrance. (Courtesy of Tom Brennan.)

ONTARIO AND WESTERN RAILROAD BRIDGE AND MAPLEWOOD CEMETERY. Here is the Ontario and Western Railroad Bridge, where the tracks pass just west of the historic Maplewood Cemetery. Maplewood is the oldest cemetery in the city, with graves dating back to the early 1830s. The cemetery experienced some difficult times in the late 20th century, but it has recently been taken over by the city and a newly formed cemetery preservation society that has begun to restore this historic treasure.

CULM PILES. Coal has not been mined in this area in over 50 years; the last coal breakers burned down or were demolished more than 20 years ago. However, gigantic, man-made mountains of black rock and dust remind Carbondaleans of their industrial roots. Included in these piles is the material that the breaker boys picked out of the mined coal one piece at a time. These black deserts are literally stained with the blood, sweat, and tears of Carbondale's ancestors, and when they finally, completely disappear, the last remnants of the industry that built Carbondale will have vanished.

Seven

MEMORABLE EVENTS

What constitutes a memorable event? Is it something dramatic, tragic, unique, or on a grand scale? It may be any of these things, but one thing is for sure, it is an event that leaves an impression. The following chapter defines memorable events as those happenings that witnesses will always remember, and which become stories that are passed on to subsequent generations to such a degree that those who were not there feel as connected to the event as those who were.

Using this definition, many events would qualify for inclusion in this text. Given the limitations of available space (as well as the lack of a photographic record for many events), the author has again chosen a few events to represent the many that could not be included.

FLOODS. Geographically speaking, Carbondale is the perfect place to put a town if the goal is for it to be flooded. It is located at the bottom of a valley with a narrow river running through it, fed by several tributaries. Extensive deforestation of the steep surrounding hillsides in an area that frequently gets more rain than Seattle also contributes to the problem. Consequently, there has been a flood every few years throughout the history of the city. These two pictures show some of the more dramatic examples of that flooding. In the picture above, the Delaware and Hudson roundhouse is being threatened by the overflowing Lackawanna River, and the photograph below shows a large automobile swept into the front yard of a home by swiftly moving waters.

THE CARBONDALE CYCLONE. This rare weather event for the area struck the northwest edge of town near Dundaff Street in 1903. As can be seen in this photograph, a group of residents from the neighborhood examines a house that was partially moved off its foundation, causing severe damage.

FLOOD-DAMAGED MINES. Floodwaters can be particularly damaging to the local economy when one of the biggest industries involves digging extensive tunnels deep into the earth. Here are piles of debris and washed-out rails near a mine opening. Some mines would never reopen after severe flooding; others might be closed for a year or more until the water subsided or could be pumped out.

WORLD WAR I WELCOME HOME PARADE. In September 1919, huge crowds lined the streets for a massive welcome home parade to honor U.S. servicemen and servicewomen returning from war overseas. At the time, this was the single biggest celebration ever held in the history of the city. As seen in these two pictures, the entire town was decorated with American flags and patriotic symbols. There were numerous bands, vehicles, and even floats in the parade, and the parade route was sometimes three or four deep with spectators.

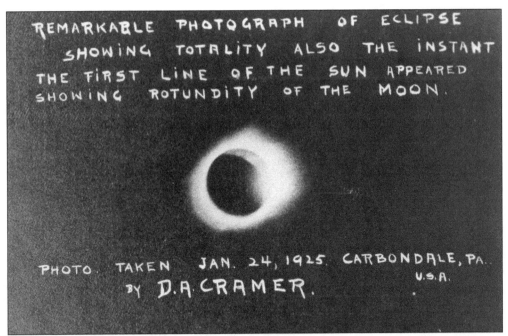

ECLIPSE. The inscription on this photograph says it all. If this photograph was remarkable in 1925, it seems even more remarkable today, looking back at the photography equipment that was in use at the time. D. A. Cramer was a professional photographer who worked in Carbondale for at least six decades.

WORLD WAR II WELCOME HOME PARADE. In 1946, the citizens of Carbondale had the occasion to once again welcome home their sons and daughters after victory had been achieved in Europe and the Pacific.

THE 1955 FIRE. In February 1955, a fire started in the Big Chief Market near the intersection of Main Street and Salem Avenue. The five-alarm fire would burn for more than 24 hours. It destroyed or damaged 17 buildings, injured five firefighters, and the town's damage was estimated at $3 million. (Courtesy of Tom Brennan.)

ANTHRACITE HOTEL FIRE. In the winter of 1974, the historic Anthracite Hotel burned down. The multi-alarm blaze was particularly difficult to fight because of bitter cold temperatures. By the time the fire was out, the entire area was covered with thick ice, and several fire trucks were frozen in place and could not be moved until they were thawed out. (Courtesy of Tom Brennan.)

MAIN STREET FIRES. These two dramatic blazes occurred at different ends of Main Street more than a decade apart and had dramatically different results. The above photograph shows a fire from the early 1990s at the corner of North Main Street and Salem Avenue. Although the third floor was completely gutted and the second and first floors were damaged, the building was ultimately restored and to this day still houses businesses and apartments. The photograph at right was the old Majestic Theatre on South Main Street and Seventh Avenue in 2005. The building threatened a seven-story apartment building for senior citizens next door to it. The theater was a complete loss, while the apartment building escaped with only minor damage. (Both, courtesy of Tom Brennan.)

119

CARBONDALE CENTENNIAL CELEBRATION. From September 17 to 20, 1951, Carbondale hosted an enormous 100th birthday party. A large-scale Broadway-style musical production was put on at Russell Park every night, there was a continuous street carnival, and parades were held daily with a massive parade on Saturday to cap things off. The picture above shows a commemorative pin that was one of several different items sold to raise money for the celebration. The photograph below shows some of the estimated 75,000 people that jammed the streets for the big parade.

CENTENNIAL PARADE. The crowds were not disappointed. This parade was one of the biggest ever seen in the area. Over 7,500 participants in every conceivable category represented communities from all over the area. These photographs show two different types of participants: the above photograph shows a fire company's women's auxiliary unit. The picture below shows one of the many elaborate floats that appeared in the parade. This particular float for Mills Brothers Hardware traces the Mills family's history in Carbondale back to 1829. (Above, courtesy of Robert McDonnell.)

THE FIRE DOWN BELOW.
Mine fires were fairly
common occurrences in coal
mining areas and were not
usually viewed as anything
more than a nuisance.
Unfortunately, the fire that
started in the abandoned
mine tunnels under the west
side of Carbondale in the
mid-1940s changed all of
that. The fire had worked its
way deep into a labyrinth of
often unmapped chambers,
most of which were under
a residential area. In 1952,
an elderly couple was killed
in their home by carbon
monoxide gas. The state
and federal governments
finally stepped in, bought
out all the homeowners in
the affected area, and began
a massive excavation to dig
out the fire in 1963. The
project would take years and
would eventually move more
earth than the building
of the Panama Canal.

A CITY ON FIRE

For 17 years the people of Carbondale, Pa., have lived in fear. Raging fires sweep through abandoned coal mines under the town. Deadly gases seeping into homes have killed townspeople in their sleep. Only the digging of giant pits can save the community.

By C. P. GILMORE

Photographs by Robert Huntzinger

A crackling blaze rises from the caverns of the earth and casts an eerie light in the midst of Carbondale. Fire threatened to destroy the town.

NATIONAL ATTENTION. During the massive operation to dig out the mine fire, Carbondale received a good deal of national media attention. This is the title page of a feature article that appeared in the September 7, 1963, issue of *The Saturday Evening Post*. The August 10, 1959, issue of *Time* also ran a science article on the Carbondale mine fire.

A CITY ON THE EDGE. This dramatic photograph, which appeared in the same issue of *The Saturday Evening Post*, was one of many captured throughout this huge undertaking. It also illustrates the danger that the entire city was facing. When the fire was finally isolated, it was discovered that it was only a few yards from spreading into a different network of tunnels that stretched under the downtown business district and a large portion of the east side residential area. If this project had been delayed by even a few more weeks, it might have meant the destruction of most of the city.

THE CARBON-D-ALIEN. On November 9, 1974, a group of teenage boys reported seeing a light streak across the sky over Russell Park in Carbondale and crash into a silt pond just south of the park. A light could be seen glowing under the water when the police arrived to investigate, and people began to spread the word that a UFO had crashed into the pond. Chaos ensued. The above photograph shows one of several volunteer fire companies on the scene who attempted to drain the pond. The draining was unsuccessful, but a scuba diver finally went into the pond and retrieved an old mining lantern, very similar to the one pictured at right. Later on, one of the original teenage witnesses admitted to throwing the lantern in the pond to scare his little sister. Before this drama had finally played out, several hundred people had swarmed to the area, rumors were flying all over, and to this day some people still claim that there was something else down in that murky water. Carbondale now has its very own urban legend. (Above, courtesy of John Uram.)

BICENTENNIAL PARADE. Carbondale's 125th anniversary coincided with America's bicentennial in 1976. This called for a celebration to rival the one in 1951, and the Pioneer City pulled out all the stops. Once again, a week of festivities was scheduled, with everything leading up to a massive parade on Saturday. These two pictures are from that parade, which featured marching units, floats, antique cars, local dignitaries, fire companies, and military units.

PAGEANT '76. Also as in 1951, a large-scale Broadway-style gala production was put on at Russell Park every night. The production told the history of Carbondale and the United States through song, dance, poetry, and skits. At right is a copy of the program cover for the production. Below is a photograph taken at one of the performances, where a group of actors portrayed the original native inhabitants of the region. This image brings this story full circle back to where it began, before the first settlers arrived in this Pioneer City.

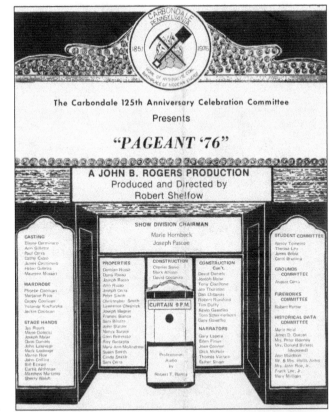

The Carbondale 125th Anniversary Celebration Committee

Presents

"PAGEANT '76"

A JOHN B. ROGERS PRODUCTION
Produced and Directed by
Robert Shelfow

SHOW DIVISION CHAIRMAN
Marie Hornbeck
Joseph Pascoe

CURTAIN 9 P.M.

Visit us at
arcadiapublishing.com

CPSIA information can be obtained
at www.ICGtesting.com
Printed in the USA
LVHW102135100920
665659LV00007B/27